UP THE CASTLE AND BEYOND

We're a' Jock Tamson's Bairns

Ray Kelly

Table of Contents

When Ray Kelly asked me to edit the text of her book 'Up the Castle and Beyond' I expected it to be a reflection of her irrepressible personality, and I was not disappointed. Her words tumbled onto the page as she recorded her thoughts and experiences of her childhood and teenage years in Burntisland. I found it to be enormously interesting and was amazed to find out what she and her young companions had been up to in Burntisland. My job turned out not to be a normal edit, correcting a few spelling and grammatical errors. Instead, I found myself finding suitable verbs for sentences, which Ray had omitted in her desire to get her thoughts quickly onto the page, and querying things that I didn't understand. At the same time, I was intent on ensuring that her style remained her own. When we sat down together to discuss my suggestions, we spent an hilarious time reliving her childhood. I had never imagined that Burntisland was like that.

Her book is a joyous recollection of her childhood and relates how she and her young companions spent their time together. Ray was in her 80th year when she wrote her book but her recollections are clear and make you feel that you were actually there. We meet people she knew, not just her young friends, but also adults who played a role in their lives. The book will be of particular interest to people who know Burntisland well, but will also appeal to people generally.

Ray has also included in her book, songs she has written to support the events she has recorded, and she has entered chords for guitar players. Ray is a very accomplished performer of her songs and I am sure we will hear her singing them in various venues.

It has been a pleasure working with her on her book and I believe it is a welcome addition to our understanding of life in Fife.

Iain Gray

Cellardyke

'Up the Castle and Beyond' skilfully weaves together Ray's cherished memories with moments of delightful creativity, ranging from poetry to songs. The author's vivid recollections take readers on an enchanting journey, painting a vivid tapestry of emotions and adventures.

One of the book's strengths lies in its ability to evoke a strong sense of nostalgia, allowing readers to relive Ray's most treasured moments alongside her. The writing is evocative, transporting the reader to the settings and scenes described with vivid detail. This immersion enhances the reading experience and fosters a deeper connection with the author's memories.

The inclusion of various creative outlets, such as poetry and songs adds an extra layer of depth to the narrative. These interludes provide glimpses into Ray's inner world and further enrich the storytelling. They serve as windows into the author's soul, allowing readers to appreciate her artistic expression and understand the profound impact these forms of activity have had on her life.

The book excels in the ability to balance introspection with engaging storytelling. While Ray's personal reflections and introspective moments offer insight into her thoughts and emotions, they never overpower the narrative flow. The pacing is well maintained, ensuring a captivating reading experience that keeps readers eager to discover what lies beyond each page.

Overall, 'Up the Castle and Beyond' is a truly engaging book that beautifully captures the essence of cherished memories and showcases the author's creative talents. It offers readers a heartfelt journey, rich with emotions, evocative descriptions and artistic expression. It is a must-read for those who appreciate the beauty of personal narratives interwoven with creativity.

Gemma Grant
English Teacher
Kent

DEDICATION

Dedicated to my parents, my husband, my sisters, (genuine Jock Tamson's bairns) my family and my grandchildren, especially Fern, who always used to say, "Gran, tell me about things that happened when you were young."

I and many more folk wish they had sat down with their parents and asked them exactly that.

Last but not least, to the resilient bunch of Castle Arabs I had the greatest pleasure to meet.

Especially Sandra, Sheila, Jem, Heather, Lauren, Gaynor, Linda, Theresa, Bill, Tom, Kathleen, Marion, Ellen and George.

I was truly in the right place at the right time.

ACKNOWLEDGEMENTS

I couldn't have made this journey without the help of some very special people.

Firstly, my guardian angel Iain Gray who has supported me from the very beginning of this amazing journey. A true scholar and a gentleman.

We did have an hilarious time discussing the "goings on" in Burntisland in the good old days. Thank you Iain for being my mentor and chivvying me on when I was procrastinating.

To Gemma Grant who gave such a wonderful review of my story. I thank you sincerely.

To Author, Sharon Brownlie and Jennie at Main Point Books who gave of their time and experience, and helped with the final formatting. Just when I was beginning to despair.

To Author Dave Henderson who gave of his experience and help at the outset.

The group Fife Writes was an encouraging group to belong to and provided a platform to perform my original songs and gave me the confidence to read aloud my written work. This was something I hadn't done before but found it uplifting.

It was a haven of peace and tranquillity at Kirkcaldy Central Library where I worked on my book for many days. The staff became friends and were so very helpful and accommodating. Also, the soup, coffee and Danish pastries provided the sustenance required to continue working on my story.

To Adam Smith, (actually his marble bust) who watched over me while I wrestled with reams of paper, as the memories came tumbling forth.

To my friends and family who have awaited the end result, especially to Fern who inspired me to write it when she always asked" tell me stories about when you were young Gran."

Thank you all most sincerely

UP THE CASTLE AND BEYOND

PREFACE

I wrote this book in my 80th year as I can remember
vividly my childhood years (not too vivid regarding
what I did yesterday!).

I remember the sights, the sounds, the smells, the
sheer freedom of growing up in the mid to late 1940's
and early 1950's in Burntisland.

Every family was in the same boat, struggling to
survive, working their fingers to the bone to keep the
boat afloat, or the publican's bank balance healthy.

A chap (knock) on the house door, "Can my mum
borrow a cup of sugar?"... neighbours helped one
another out. Life was hard for our parents, but it was
good for us bairns who wouldn't have changed it for
the world. It has stood us in great stead to overcome
life's many obstacles.

No home phones, no internet, no central heating, no car. None of that mattered. We had our freedom, we had respect for our elders, we were taught discipline at school.

I'm so glad I reached for my iPad and got everything I remembered typed into notes, or the stories would have been lost forever.

My original songs and words regarding my childhood are peppered throughout, if you fancy playing and singing along.

Take time to sit with your children and grandchildren and tell them your stories.

I do hope you enjoy

UP THE CASTLE AND BEYOND...

Chapter One
Up The Castle

As children, we lived "Up the Castle." Now you may wonder… "Up the Castle," what does that mean? I suppose it was because you had to walk uphill and across a bridge with battlements leading to two magnificent arches, then, on the left was Rossend Castle, standing derelict, in its own grounds. If anyone asked you where you lived, the reply would be "Up the Castle."

The first street one encountered was Melville Gardens facing the castle. This area was considered the "posh end." What were the stables for the castle in olden days lay across your path, with a nice grassy triangle in front with a lovely red telephone box, where you could nip in to see if the previous user had forgotten to take their returned pennies. "Press button A to speak… button B to have your money returned if no answer."

Then, on to Shepherd Crescent, which was still considered "posh."

It was "The Cut" which separated that posh end from the reality of life in Rossend Terrace. Folks used to say, "you'll need a passport to enter if you dare," but there was something magical about that transition through "The Cut."

Have you ever tried to remember who lived where when you were young? In the block next to ours, there was a sea captain, as well as an old couple, the old woman dressed all in black and always at the window watching all who passed by. Unknown to me then, the old couple were my future husband's grandparents. Granny Catherine Flannigan had said to her grandson, "See that lassie Thomson, she would make a lovely girlfriend for you," and lo-and-behold the rest is history!

The street was arranged in a very large oval. We lived in the very highest block of four at the top end of the Terrace. Our house and a few more had impressive battlement architecture around the front entrance doors. There were thirty steps up to our three bedroom flat. The house door key was on a piece of string and you put your hand through the letterbox to retrieve it. The inside stair was unwelcoming. Dark brown painted steps with wee oblongs of linoleum stuck to the centre of each tread. The walls were brown, and stippled with cream paint, courtesy of Burntisland Shipbuilding Company, and the ingenious make do and mend decorating skills of my mother.

Most of the Castle residents worked in the shipyard and depending on the colours of the ship being built, milk bottles or any kind of suitable receptacles were used to smuggle out the paint among other things, so a vast majority of the kitchens up the castle were painted to match the ship!

Chapter Two

Freedom

Much freedom was afforded to us kids. Those were the days when, at a fairly young age, we were free as the birds. Meeting with our pals and being out all day playing games in the fresh air, more often than not, in the middle of the road as there were few cars around.

It was exciting when the visiting grocer, baker, complete with horse and cart, lemonade lorry, ice cream van, rag man and fish man suddenly appeared in Rossend Terrace.

No car, no television, no phone, no Facebook. Just imagine! We made our own entertainment.

Two pals turning the heavy washing rope as a skipping rope was a favourite. The chant, "High" "low" "dolly" "pepper" comes to mind with the skipping game, and woe betide if that heavy rope caught your face as you misjudged the timing. There would be as many as twenty kids, all playing, getting their exercise and wonderful fresh air. We played at sketches, nowadays they call it hopscotch. We chalked the pavement and used the kiwi polish tin as the slider. We played games of "levoy," (hide and seek) someone being 'het'. "You're het," meaning it's your turn to stand at the lamppost and count to a hundred while the rest of us hid, and you had to come looking for us, often in the evening darkness, which made it all the more exciting.

"Changing scraps" was a favourite and quite an obsessive pastime. You tried to collect whole sets and paste them into a scrapbook. You could swap your doublers with your pals, sitting on their doorstep after school. Paper scraps were sets of cutout images of, for example, children holding different toys, assorted floral images, animals, plump angels, etc. I can still see visions of these plump angels with their arms crossed, leaning on fluffy clouds. "I'll swap you that one."

We greatly anticipated a wedding in Rossend Terrace. The big black taxi rolled up and the bride emerged with her father. We were so excited and watched carefully to see on which side the bride's father was seated. He was the one with the "scatter." It was customary and considered good luck to throw money from the taxi window as the bride left the family home. As the taxi drove slowly away, the pushing and shoving would begin when the coins were thrown out of the taxi window onto the street with fingers being stood upon. Standing on the shiny coins first was a good strategy, as it was a quick way to secure them before picking them up, then hightailing it down to St. Columba's Church for yet another "scatter" when the newlyweds left as Mr. and Mrs. The sweetie shops were the next destination.

The gang would have a meeting to decide their next adventure. Gathering in the grounds of the derelict Rossend Castle, just as darkness was falling, instilled a feeling of fear, excitement and trepidation. The window at the side was accessible if you climbed up on your friend's shoulders. It was like a circus act, with three bodies supporting the ascent. Once in, it was very dangerous, as the floor had collapsed completely and there were only rotten joists to stand on. We were hoping to see the ghost of Mary, Queen of Scots, as she had spent a few nights in the Castle. Tenants in the houses opposite, in Melville Gardens were always on the lookout, and would phone the police. We had a lookout too, who would warn us if the police van approached, and we would make a hasty retreat out another window at the rear.

We were outdoors from dawn till dusk. Changed days indeed, for children nowadays, their parents always wary of the dangers present in society. We were so lucky, and had the best ever apprenticeship, growing up with that sense of adventure and freedom. Those were the "good old days." indeed.

Chapter Three

The Monks Walk

The Monks Walk ran along the back of our house, aptly named, as one can imagine an order of Monks walking along this tranquil narrow path in bygone days. A glance over the wall provided a panoramic view of Burntisland Shipbuilding Company far below. There was a corrugated shelter part way along, which served as a private place for the older courting couples to enjoy. Our thoughts hadn't turned to any such goings on. Instead, we had fun swinging from the metal beams which held up the structure. We were agile wee monkeys!

En route to the Point, one encountered the slippy slope, so called because of its steepness and slippery muddy surface, if it had been raining. Great courage was required to negotiate it, and often, as not the descent was on your bottom. The ascent was always difficult, hauling yourself up with the help of your friends and the ivy, which was growing in abundance.

The Castle Arabs, as we affectionately call ourselves, had built a gang hut halfway down the slope, with some corrugated sheeting we had acquired. Many a rainy day we would gather in our very own gang hut, and put the world to rights, then wonder how on earth we were going to get back up that slippery slope. A sturdy rope, courtesy of a "friend" was tied to the tree and you could swing out, right over the shipyard if you were brave enough.

Wee Sydney Baxter and his mum,
Kathleen, Bill and Tom George. John Tulloch and his mum,
Billy Braid and one other lad.

Wee lad ready to swing out over the shipyard

Photo credit: The Malone family

Chapter Four

The Point, Sea Coal, Soot And A Monkey

"Oh, the happy memories of the Point."

On reaching the end of the path, one encountered the most fabulous view of the Firth of Forth, and The Forth Railway Bridge in the distance. The other two bridges hadn't been built then. Rocks and shoreline beckoned, with nooks and crannies to explore, and to the right, a long concrete breakwater which bordered the red pond. The red pond was where The British Aluminium Company deposited red ore. It was also where the Castle bonfire was erected and invariably set alight prematurely by the "Silverbarton Gang." The "Castle Arabs" duly responded.

Fearless, fast, fit, and agile as gazelles, we descended the steep rocky slope, instinctively knowing the foot placements which were etched in our memory banks. Happy hours on end were spent at the Point, and we came across a naturist who would sunbathe in the nude and chewed seaweed. Haha, we would lie on our stomachs on the rocks high above and peer down at him and have a good giggle. When it was low tide, you could access the shore round by the shipyard wall. This was where all the sea coal was washed in from Seafield, and where half the residents of the Castle would congregate with prams, and other receptacles, to gather the free fuel to keep the draughty houses cosy in the winter months, although most of the heat went up the lum. No central heating in those days, and if the fire hadn't been on to heat the back boiler for the warm water, a kettle was boiled for the family's ablutions. We were tough cookies, and no worries about paying extortionate heating bills. Times were hard enough. It's just incredible that, fast forward almost eighty years, and folks are still struggling financially.

Mr Bett was "the coupon man." He would deliver the Vernon's and Littlewoods Football Coupons to be completed. Our dad would mark crosses against the various football teams he guessed would be the winners. The coupons were collected again each Friday night. It was a ritual at 5 p.m. every Saturday teatime to listen to the wireless (radio) to check the results. Every family dreamed of winning and having their lives changed forever. One neighbour did win a good few thousand pounds.

The coal man did a roaring trade too and he must have cursed when our order went in. He had to carry the sacks from his cart all the way up the thirty plus steps to be deposited in a cupboard in the hall. The coal dust must have coated our lungs. From our window high above, we always kept a wary eye on him, checking that we got the correct number of bags we were paying for. From time to time, in fact quite regularly, a sooty, burning smell filled your nostrils, and the black reek signalled that a scrunched up newspaper had been set alight and thrust up a chimney in Rossend Terrace. This set the soot on fire and did the trick, and saved paying for the sweep. If you ordered the sweep, there were usually two of them. One on the roof with the brush, and one kneeling by the fireplace, holding a manky strong linen sheet against the aperture in the tiled grate. The sweep on the roof shouted "beeeeeeee" down the chimney to warn his workmate down below of the impending deluge of soot. It took a week to dust all the black soot which escaped and managed to cover every surface in the living room and beyond.

Yes, it was a tiled grate the council had installed. Very posh we thought. The original fireplaces had been the black leaded ones with an oven at the side. Our friends down the road had kept theirs. Bobby, their father, had been in the merchant navy with my father, and brought this petite monkey back from one of his trips. I can still see it's cute wee face to this day. The oven at the side of the fire was its home and kept it warm during the cold winters.

My father made a cleek (a long, metal L-shaped contraption). This was used to help turn over the large heavy rocks, at the Point, under which the parkins hid. They were large crabs with vicious pincers. They were plentiful, and would be placed in the deep sink in the scullery, until they were boiled and we got the claws and a needle to howk oot the white meat, which was delicious. It's really the only time I can remember my father taking me out anywhere. He was working for hours in the shipyard.

Chapter Five

The Shippy

In the late 1940s and 1950s, 500 men would make their way through the gates at 7.30 a.m. each morning when the horn blew. Most were local, and from the surrounding area, popping into Gilmour's paper shop for their reading material and "baccy" first. The town was a hive of prosperity.

Every night as we lay in bed, the room was lit up by flashes from the welding torches, and sounds of the hammers banging on metal as the men worked through the night.

Nice fat pay packets on a Friday, but sadly, the local publicans got the biggest whack.

Some wives would be standing at the gate on pay day waiting for the men to finish, to make sure they got the housekeeping money. The men got wise and clocked out early, went to the pub at lunchtime and the poor women were left to struggle to feed their families.

A fine shortcut from the High Street to access Rossend Terrace, was by the Shippy stairs which led to the Monks Walk. Many a time bairns would stand at the top of the stairs waiting for their dads to appear after a hard shift. Those were the days when you had your dinner at 12 noon and your tea at teatime, 5 o'clock.

My very first job was in the Shipyard offices. A great experience except when the boss in the office took away my eraser, as I was making too many typing errors!

At the entrance, a posh revolving door led into a beautiful wood panelled reception area, and sometimes you took a turn on the reception desk. I felt quite important when that happened.

There was a raised curved area facing the dock, known as the half moon. This was a perfect vantage point to watch the visiting dignitaries and the ships being launched. The heavy chains would rattle behind as the ships came off the slipway to slow them down. The ship launches were enjoyed by the vast majority of Burntisland residents.

It was Sir Wilfred Ayre, Naval Architect and Banker (1890-1971) who, with his brother, Sir Amos Ayre founded Burntisland Shipbuiding Company in 1918.

I wrote a song about my father working in the Shipyard. It's called Jock Tamson's Bairns, and my sisters and I are truly Jock Tamson's Bairns.

Born Ray Hutton Thomson

Father John Thomson

I've got the birth certificate to prove it!

Jock Tamson's Bairns.

A song by Ray Kelly

Key of D

Verse 1

    D   A   D

When we were young, we sat on the floor, our daddy

                 A

would dry our hair

    D   A   C.   D

Soaking wet, dripping water, all the curls would appear,

C.   D.   C.   D

No such things as hair dryers, a towel was all he'd use

         C.   D

With a spitting sound coming from the fire

        A   D

I've got the Rossend Terrace Blues

        A   D

I've got the Rossend Terrace Blues

Verse 2

    D   A   G   D

Our daddy was a crane driver, in the shipyard down below

    D   A   G   D

The horn would hoot and 500 men, to work each day would go

       C   D   C

Their pieces made up, a can for the brew, wee fires lit

    D
everywhere
      C.   D   A.
The shipyard smells of oil and rust, coiled ropes, strong brew
     D
and dust
      A   D
Coiled ropes, strong brew and dust.

Chorus.
        C   D   C   D
We're aw Jock Tamson's bairns, something we never forgot
       C   D   C   D
Cause this old world is slowly, slowly going to pot

Verse Three
D   A   G   D
The horn would hoot at twelve o'clock, time for dinner now
 D   A   G   D
Up the shipyard stairs so steep, sweat dripping off the brow
 C   D   C   D
A plate o' soup, then back again for the afternoon shift
    C   D   A   D
The metal dangling from the ropes, "Hey Jock, we need a lift"

Verse Four.
 D   A   G
Five o'clock and us bairnies three would stand there just a
 D
waiting,

```
 D                    A          G      D
at the top of the shippy stairs, in wild anticipation
C                    D          C          D
See who'd spy their father first, limping up the stairs
 C                    D                    A
Polio got him at an early age you've got to work or you don't
      D
get paid
              A                    D
You've got to work or you don't get paid
```

Chorus.
```
      C                D      C              D
We're aw Jock Tamson's bairns, something we never forgot
      C                D      C          D
Cause  this old world is slowly, slowly going to pot
```

Verse Five
```
  D          A      G          D
Plenty of overtime, so back to work again
 D          A                G          D
working well into the night, the sky so very bright
C                    D      C              D
Lit up with the welding torches, hammers banging on metal
  C              D              A
We couldn't sleep for all that noise, but the men were in fine
  D
fettle
   A                D
The men were in fine fettle.
```

Verse Six

    D   A   G

We daughters three just could not sleep, we had made a plan wi'

    D

oor dad

D   A   G   D

Three flashes of our scullery light, and dad would flash us back,

      C   D   C   D

Wi' his torch, from his crane, towering ower the yard,

 C   D   A   D

it made us so excited sweet memories ignited

       A   D

Sweet memories ignited

Chorus.

      C   D   C   D

We're aw Jock Tamson's bairns, something we never forgot

 C   D   C   D

For this old world is slowly, slowly going to pot

We're a' Jock Tamson's Bairns

Ray and the twins, Sandra and Sheila

With our dad

Chapter Six

You take the High Road and I'll take the Low Road

A jam piece and a bottle of water was all you needed on a bright sunny summer day.

Heading for Rossend Point and the breakwater, seemed a very long way when you were wee. Walking along the breakwater wall and jumping over the sewer which was half-way along, and counting these plentiful creamy coloured balloon type things which were floating on the water (birth control), relieved the boredom of the walk.

The Breakwater

You could walk along a rather rocky shore to get to our destination, but it seemed more exciting to cross the railway. Listening intently for any trains approaching, one by one we took off like greyhounds out of a trap and scrambled across the tracks and the rough stones in between them. We had no inkling of the dangers. We were Castle Arabs.

The signalman in the box not too far off would call the police, but we were well along the Low Road by then. The High Road was the main road linking Burntisland to Aberdour.

The Low Road coastal path was narrow, with sweet wild strawberries and shiny juicy black brambles growing in abundance, along the route. The path then widened, and this was where an entrepreneur had set up a tent selling cold drinks and snacks.

There was an orchard with numerous apple trees, laden with fruits, as we neared our destination. This was too much of a temptation, so a wee leg up over the wall provided the Castle Arabs with their vitamin C.

Our destination was in sight - Starleyburn, with a wonderful wild expanse of seeding long grasses, sedges, bluebells, lilac thrift, colourful butterflies and again the sea and the cliffs, all of which were such a big part of our childhood.

We would lie on our bellies peering over the rocks to the sea below witnessing dense shoals of silvery mackerel swimming near the surface.

We had probably eaten our pieces and drunk our water, but we knew of a source of fresh, well maybe not so fresh water. Along past the lovely waterfall was a pipe with a wee hole in the top. If you covered the front with your hand, the water would spout out of the hole, allowing you to quench your thirst and fill up your empty bottle. We didn't even think what that water had passed through on its way down the slope!

The Bluebell Wood was nearby, so a scramble up

through the trees meant that you could pick some bluebells to take home for your mum. The gooey sap seeped out of the stem ends, and they were half dead by the time you got home. It's such a pity that now huge metal gates prevent folks from visiting Starleyburn. The "Keep Out" sign makes me so sad, as Starleyburn was our childhood playground and gave us so much pleasure. I would love to savour the memories of being there just one more time. Anyone got a boat?

It's a lovely walk along the Low Road to the waterfall and the pipe is still there, but there is a much safer way to access this hidden gem, without crossing the railway.

The Water Pipe

Free as the Wind
A poem by Ray Kelly

Are you coming out to play with the rest,
along the Monks walk is the best.
We can have some fun, be free,
Free as the wind.

Hit the shelter first above the shipyard,
write on the walls, swing on the bars.
No one to reprimand us,
be free, free as the wind.

We can climb the wall, slide down the slippery slope
to the corrugated shelter we all built.
A swing on the rope over the shipyard,
scary if you dare.

A scramble down the rocks at the Point,
like gazelles light of foot,

Running amongst the wild dog rose and slippery
seaweed,

Free as the seabird.

The breakwater next to Starleyburn,

the railway halts us in our path.

We're castle Arabs 1, 2, 3, let's cross,

then picking wild strawberries along the narrow path.

Sunny days at Starleyburn, with jam pieces, water
bottles,

on our bellies, peering down into the briny,

The shoals of mackerel darting swiftly

below the surface.

Those carefree days of youth back then,

the kids of today will never know,

Were the best days of our lives,

the best days of our lives.

Chapter Seven
All the fun of the fair

Andrew Young, (1854-1925) was a commercial photographer, and prolific artist. He painted local scenes. Wonderful large compositions, including "All the Fun of the Fair" and "Bridge of Life." All the fun of the fair depicted Burntisland residents, sometimes appearing twice as different characters. My grandfather appeared as a soldier and also a boxer in the ring.

Some of Andrew Young's paintings are on show in The Burgh Chambers. He also painstakingly restored many of the panels in the historic Parish Church of St Columba.

The fairground, or shows, still visit the Links for a few months each year.

During the fairground stay, the Highland Games were, and still are, held on the Links, a very busy day for the town with folks visiting from far and near. Visitors would arrive in red double decker buses, colourful streamers billowing from the open windows. Quite a sight to behold! Lots going on with Highland dancing, tossing the caber, the Binn Hill Race, and the greasy pole to name but a few.

It was easy for young children to get lost in the crowds. Their mothers would be panicking and were so relieved to hear the messages over the loudspeaker, to say their child was safe and well and being looked after in the marquee.

It was Vincie from Rossend Terrace, (from doon the bottom end), who was the champion of the greasy pole. A tall pole was erected in Harbour Place, and on the top was pinned a ten pound note and two five pound notes – a lot of money at the time. The pole was covered in grease to make it all the more difficult to climb, and the first one to the top won ten pounds, and so on. It was such fun with vast crowds of spectators watching as the contestants got so far up the pole then slid down, only to try again and again. Vincie, our "Castle Champion" always won. Woe betide if you were standing nearby, as the participants threw handfuls of the grease down on the onlookers.

At the end of the day, once the trips had departed, a few entrepreneurs would rake about all the refuse bins for the empty Plummer's lemonade bottles. If you returned the empties, you could make a fortune. That was possibly the beginning of recycling as we know it!

The fair itself comprised bingo stalls where your mum saved the vouchers until you had enough for one of the many prizes. Oh, maybe a new pair of sheets or a new frying pan.

We always made a beeline for the penny machines. "A penny" these big brown heavy metal coins which you placed in the slot and a metal marble appeared. You spun it round and would try to get it into the inner row of cups. Haha the metal pins were tightly placed there, so the marble bounced down into the lose hole every time. "Never mind, we can check and see if anyone has forgotten to take their winnings from the apertures at the base."

The waltzers consisted of a number of carriages which spun freely. As the cars revolved the floor of the ride undulated over a fast moving track.

The balcony round the waltzers was a great meeting place for kids, with loud music and the frantic spinning of the carriages. Sometimes the workers would jump on the back of your carriage and make it spin even faster. They were quick to check under the seats the minute you vacated them hoping what little cash you had, had dropped out in the frenzy.

The Hook a Duck stall looked so exciting with all the prizes displayed in the centre - prizes that hardly anybody won. Giant teddy bears, huge dolls and goldfish. Oh yes, the goldfish!! Mine lasted a day before it went horizontal and pale and floated motionless in its new glass bowl.

Not much luck with pets either. Joey, our yellow and green budgerigar, escaped out of the partly opened window, and was never seen again. He was a "pretty boy," and we had just bought him a load of millet spray from Syme's shop on the High Street. We were devastated. I digress… back to the "Hook a Duck" stall.

You were given a rod with a hook on the end, and had to hook one of the wee yellow plastic ducks swimming around in the water. All had numbers on the base, but so many numbers were not winners. "Sorry, you've lost?" said the stall-holder. I suppose the travelling folk had to make a living, and their presence brought much fun and excitement to us kids during the summer months.

Chapter Eight

Sustenance

The mobile grocer, the lemonade lorry, the ice cream man, the store baker, the milkman, the rag man, the coal man, all came round Rossend Terrace. What great service back then. Oh, the rag man - with all the rags piled up on the flat cart drawn by his horse, and those wonderful red balloons, tied to the side, moving gently in the wind were such a temptation for a youngster. I seem to remember getting into trouble, and acquiring a few red balloons for trading my dad's cardigan!!!

A visit to the ice cream man, with your Pyrex bowl meant it would be filled with delicious ice cream which cost sixpence, and an extra penny for a pile of wafers, which meant lovely ice cream sliders for the whole family.

The fish man's cry to inform us he was in the vicinity was "hurry, hurry, fresh fish here!"

You also had the choice to shop down the High Street. Your mum wrote out the message line and handed it to the shop assistant who made up your grocery order.

The food seemed to have real taste too in those days. Certain commodities were rationed and everyone had their ration book with weekly coupons, to hand over to the shop assistant.

It was the store baker, Willie Vallance, who came round with his horse and cart, and he always had a fag hanging out his mouth as he pulled out the board with all the goodies. Cakes, Paris buns, coconut buns, triangular bran scones and half loaves to name but a few. We fought over the heels (the end slices) of the store bread. It was lovely toasted with butter. Yes, we had butter, but no fridge. The butter was kept cool, immersed in a dish of water in the pantry in the scullery. There was a pulley overhead to dry the clothes which were permeated with the smell of whatever was on the menu. Usually lentil soup or peas and barley. The latter was made with boiling beef and the lentil with ham. Potted meat was a staple. The haugh and napp bone were boiled for hours and the meat minced through the metal mincer which was screwed on to the wooden worktop. We three sisters took great pleasure leaning out of the scullery window, calling to the downstairs neighbour's dog, and waving the boiling beef from above. The dog was half way up the drainpipe as we dropped the tasty morsel into its open jaws!!

Willie Vallance, the Store baker, would normally stop half way down the hill. This is where the horse religiously had a "poo." Health and safety wasn't an issue back then.

The residents nearby would run with their shovels to collect it. Mrs. Gow always got there first as she lived nearest. She had the best roses in town.

"Do you remember your store number?" "Aye, 1381." Depending on how much you spent in The Burntisland Co-operative Society, periodically they paid out a dividend. You had to queue up outside the offices or down at the Co-op Hall, in Links Street and wait your turn. "Oh God, everyone would get a good tea that night." The Store as we called it had the monopoly on the High Street with other premises – a butcher, baker, shoe shop, grocers, chemist, hardware, drapers, and bakehouse in Somerville

Street. Mary Somerville (1780-1830) spent her childhood in Somerville Street.

She was a Scottish scientist, writer, and polymath. She studied mathematics and astronomy, and in 1835 she and Caroline Herschel were elected as the first female Honorary Members of the Royal Astronomical Society. She is featured on the Royal Bank of Scotland ten pound note.

All the shops had colourful sun canopies which looked really pretty, and saved the contents of their windows from melting in the summer heat. The summers were hot, with tar bubbling on the pavements, which made a terrible mess of your white sand shoes. They call them trainers now.

There were numerous bakers, The Co-op of course, Brocks at the bottom of the High Street, before they moved further up the street. Donaldsons, whose bake house was always busy in the early hours of the morning, the smell of the newly baked morning rolls was a magnet for those who had been out on the town at the various drinking establishments, or at the Palace Picture House late night horror films. "The

Midnight Movies." Millar's French cakes were a favourite, and The Green Cockatoo was real class. Page the Baker's shop was on the corner of Lothian Street and the High Street, and made the most delicious hot mince pies, oozing grease, and, peering through their window at night, you could spy a good stock of live mickey mice running around.

At Drummond's fish shop, water cascaded relentlessly down the inside of the window, much to our delight.

Anderson's the newsagent was a lovely large shop in which to have a browse, and Clayson's was another newsagent. Sid McCracken's shop was a magnet for day visitors. Here they could purchase their souvenirs and gifts to remind them of their happy visit to sunny Burntisland.

You could smell the wonderful aroma of Moller's boiled ham cooked on the premises. Across the road in Mr. Fraser the Butcher's shop, I can vividly remember the poor wee rabbits, hanging at eye level, inverted on hooks with their wee heads pointing down to the sawdust floor.

We also had Brown the Butcher, the Co-op again of

course, and Alex Graham, a few blocks along from the picture house.

Shopping was done daily for fresh butcher meat as there were few, if any refrigerators in the homes.

I used to be sent to Lows, a wonderful grocers shop, with the message line, which was handed over the counter to the assistant, and they quickly gathered your shopping together. Again, the smells were amazing. The large rounds of cheese, which were cut with a wire. The assistant fashioned your order for half a pound of butter, from the huge blocks with ridged butter pats, serrated to grip the butter and make a nice pattern.

Hays the grocer made delicious steak pies. If you so wished, they could be delivered to your home by message boys. Their bikes had big metal baskets on the front to hold the shopping orders.

Aitkens sweetie shop was opposite my grandparents' house on the High Street and sold lovely ice cream.

My favourite shop was Carrie Patterson's sweetie shop at the bottom of the High Street next to the Close where the Silver Band practised. She made the best tablet in the world, and most of our pay from the Sunday paper round was exchanged for lovely sweets.

Dandi Macari's ice cream was legendary. Delicious and colourful knickerbocker glories, banana splits and ice cream dropped into your favourite lemonade were all amazing.

Although no food was sold in Pat Stevensons the Ironmongers in Harbour Place, it deserves a mention. I can still smell the paraffin purchased to fill the black Valor Heater and it was a real chore when you were sent there with the heavy accumulator to have it charged to power your wireless. Oh, listening to Radio Luxembourg and sending away for free samples of Lincoln Beer Shampoo, which came in a wee plastic barrel. That was a pleasure indeed!

Barrels of salt herring sat outside the grocers shops, and there were ship chandler's who supplied everything for the ships docked in the harbour. The town was a hive of activity back then.

We had numerous fish and chip shops, all with high

counters. A small bag of chips cost four pence, and a large bag was sixpence, delicious, with the vinegar dripping out of the bottom of the poke.

Gilmour's paper shop was the starting off point for the Sunday mystery tours. Not much of a mystery really, because it was usually either Alva or Cupar.

All dressed in our "Sunday Best" clothes, we would wait patiently for the cream coloured Alexander's bus with the bluebird logo on the side to arrive. Everyone jostled to claim the front seats.

It was an exciting day with your high tea in a hotel. What a delight with real tablecloths and the obligatory three tier cake stand with all the lovely scones and cakes. We always spied them first and usually stuck our finger in the one we fancied. "That one's mine!" but we had to finish our fish and chips or steak pie first.

The waitresses were always very smart, dressed in black apart from their white aprons and caps. I can remember sitting in the bus, soaked to the skin as I had fallen into the pond in the park at Cupar.

Gilmour's paper shop was my first pocket money job. Delivering papers with my friend on a Sunday morning. It was the most demanding paper round in the town. We walked for miles, carrying the heavy bags filled with mainly the Sunday Post, starting off at The Castle and finishing at Kirkbank Road. The one consolation was the pay packet. The hard earned money was swiftly spent in Morris's and Simpson's fruit shops, and Carry Paterson's sweetie shop.

As we made our way home, along by the half moon, up the shippy stairs and along the Monks Walk, we were exhausted, but our bellies were full.

Chapter Nine

The Daily Dooks

The open air Bathing Pool stood at the end of the promenade by the shore and was our salvation. A season ticket was seven shillings and sixpence, and it meant unlimited entry during the summer months. I imagine every child in Burntisland possessed one. They were our passport to freedom! Parents seemed to find the money, and it kept us kids out of their hair.

Carefully laying out a towel on the bed and rolling up your swimming costume, you set off every single day to the bathing pool. We were making sure we got our money's worth.

It took roughly twenty minutes to walk there from Rossend Terrace, passing on the way, the old lady, Granny Flannigan, sitting at her window. Then through the infamous "Cut." past the red phone box and Castle, through the arches, and past the Barns with the horses and carts ready to whisk the fertiliser off to the farms.

Rather than walk the busy High Street, and it was busy, the Back Lane ran parallel to it, and gave easy access to the Links and fairground. It saved you getting caught by the photographer with his tripod stationed outside the bank. I think everyone in Burntisland will have had a photo taken by him there.

On the left hand side of the lane was a steep hill called Broomhill, aptly named because of the dense clusters of broom, gorse and brambles which were abundant. Broomhill was also the home of teachers. The Misses Simpson who lived in a big house there, as well as Mr. Moyes, a teacher at the Piscy (Episcopalian) School. On, past the Music Hall and gas works.

There were three tunnels joining the Links, this huge grassy area, to the beach and the bathing pool. Through the first tunnel, over the level crossing and there it stood, this wonderful escape from normality - the bathing pool. At the entrance there was a kiosk, where your season ticket was checked, and woe betide if you had forgotten it......it was a long walk home. There were two turnstiles, an "in" and an "out" at the side of the kiosk, and as you progressed through they made loud clicking sounds. This wonderful sight greeted you. A large pool which looked inviting because of the colour it was painted. A beautiful turquoise blue, with the sun glinting on the water surface, but appearances can be deceiving. It was freezing!!! Seawater was used and processed in the boiler room, presumably to purify it. Music was usually playing from another kiosk, and the cafe was upstairs. Galas were held with visiting groups competing in the swimming races. Water polo was a favourite to watch and you could have swimming lessons also.

Beauty competitions were often held on a Sunday, when the shapely contestants walked around the perimeter in their swimsuits. Trying to look cool and not stumble in their stiletto heels, they each held a card with a number boldly written on it, whilst being scrutinised by a panel of celebrity judges. "Slip the judge a tenner and you'll win."

Right, brace yourself for the coldest, most miserable dressing room on God's earth.

A numbered metal basket was given to you for your clothes, and a rubber wristband with a corresponding number to hand over when you stood, shivering at the counter, waiting to retrieve your clothes after your swim. I shudder to think of the next part. It was compulsory to walk through the disinfectant foot bath. Absolutely baltic, but we found a way to manoeuvre through, rather precariously balancing on the raised edge. We were Castle Arabs and, where there's a will there's a way. We learned that from experience.

Spectators could view the pool action from tiered seating areas at both sides, or from upstairs. What a view from upstairs, taking in the bay, beach, imposing Erskine Church and the magnificent backdrop of the Binn Hill.

My original watercolour painting of the beach, prom and Erskine Church

A wee sit in the sun first, then a walk down to the wooden steps at the 3 feet end. The pool sloped to 11 feet at the deep end. This was where the diving boards were, comprising the high dive, and two others, also the big chute, down which I was too scared to slide.

It took ages to become immersed. First the big toe, then down a couple of steps at a time, until the freezing water reached the top of your legs. Oh, the next bit was hard. Walking ever so slowly, as the water got deeper. Up to the waist now, but it was the arms, oxters and shoulders which were the worst. One two three. "Oh bliss, that's me under."

The backstroke was my favourite, as you didn't have to have your face in the water.

Galas were held periodically with visiting swimming clubs competing in the races. Breaststroke, backstroke and freestyle – fifty or a hundred yards. What a joy to watch. Ropes which had bits of cork attached to make them float kept the lanes orderly.

Halcyon, warm summer days at the pool

No wonder I was a skinny, with all that healthy exercise of walking, swimming, skipping and adventuring. Hesitant to come out of the water, because you knew what was in store. There were polar bears in that dressing room! The cold wind swirled all around as you shivered on that wooden board getting dressed. It was always the coldest place in Burntisland even on the warmest of days.

The next bit was really good. Upstairs to the café to visit Betty and Jock Watson for a hot blackcurrant or hot orange, and maybe a hot store pie, if your pocket money allowed. Then the long walk home with your pals. Taking a different route, past Drummond's smokehouse, where they gutted and smoked the fish, the women, in their long rubber aprons, swept the smelly fishy water out into the street. Then along Leven Street, skirting the shipyard up the shipyard steps three at a time, along the Monks Walk and eventually climbing over the fence at our back green. Home at last for a bite to eat, but not for long, before we returned to the bathing pool for another swim. We did get our money's worth.

Chapter Ten

Education

I didn't really apply myself at Burntisland Junior Secondary School. I just managed to see the light in the higher grade year and pulled my socks up, and got to Kirkcaldy High School for the 4 year intensive course, which didn't actually last four years, but was four years work condensed into one, with shorthand, bookkeeping, typing, English and arithmetic on the curriculum.

The Burntisland Junior Secondary school was a Victorian set of old buildings, scattered around the playgrounds. I "ticked" the school (played truant) a few times, not realising it would be documented on the "Report Card" - Attendance 132 out of 148!!!

The Teachers

The teachers were a mixed bunch. Miss Peatie, Miss

Shand, Miss McArthur, the English teacher, quite foreboding. Miss Toshack who taught us dressmaking, and how to iron. Miss Forsyth (Fanny) ......think her name was Francis, the music teacher was a lovely talented soul and brilliant pianist, but she definitely had her work cut out with our unruly bunch. We used to say "Oh Miss, please play us The Dambusters and The Glass Mountain." They were really long musical pieces on which she had to concentrate, whilst we had high jinks.

A particular school mate of mine was a lovely lad, but was forever getting the belt for being disruptive. He would be taken out into the middle of the room and had to extend his arms in front, and cross his hands. He was a bit of a scamp though. I remember on one occasion, just as the belt was descending, he would open his arms, and the poor teacher got hit on the leg, much to the delight of his fellow pupils. "Oh dear, forgive us Lord."

The art teacher lived by the golf course and he taught us italic writing, which we didn't pay much attention to, unfortunately. It was he who caught me and my pal June, climbing out the science block window at playtime. It was raining, and we hatched a plan to hide among the coats in the cloakroom inside, as the doors were locked during playtime. We got bored and decided to climb out of the window, and lo and behold, there was our art teacher heading to the staff room for his break!!! He caught us red-handed, midway, half a body out, balancing to reach Mother Earth. Up the stairs to the headmaster's office yet again!!

Then there was the woodwork teacher, nicknamed "Sconnie." We were sure he had a wig which resembled a scone! His classroom was adjacent to the gym hall. He would be writing on the blackboard and hear the chattering, and without turning round, throw the wooden duster into the class. Good job we were quick to duck. The classroom doors had glass panels at the top, and the boys would take a chance to peer through to the gym hall and watch the girls in their navy blue knickers and white blouses performing their physical education. The boys were reprimanded by the teacher for being "unsavoury."

I did enjoy PE, (physical education). Mr. Izzy was our teacher and was also a referee at boxing matches. He was always immaculate, dressed in his whiter than white attire.

Ropes were lowered from the ceiling, which we had to try and climb. We did handstands on the wall bars, oh, and there was that worn leather contraption called a horse you had to loup over, often with great difficulty. However, I did enjoy netball. I was help-shoot, but I have to admit, I was not very good at it. We had netball teams visiting from other schools for friendly matches. During gym and outdoor sports sessions, all pupils were segregated into groups. We had four different coloured cloth bands which you wore across your body. My band was blue, (but should have been Red for Rossend) for Dunearn, green represented Greenmount, yellow for Grange, and red for Rossend. The four houses were named after districts in Burntisland. On school sports day, we marched along Ferguson Place, James Park, and along Kirkbank Road to the grassy expanse known as Bentfield, to compete for the annual sports trophy.

The school dentist and "nit nurse" were housed in a small building off the playground.

The waiting room was clinical, and polished to the nines. It was an ordeal to visit the dentist, with the antiquated and dreaded drill, worked by a foot pedal. The nurse was on hand for any bloody playground accidents. There was an epidemic of nits in the school, and it was inevitable that eventually, everyone was cursed with these wee pests, which nestled and multiplied readily in your hair. Every pupil was sent in turn to the nit nurse. An itchy head, and the nits were soon passed around. Every mum had a bone comb at home.

It wasn't unusual to have around 40 pupils in a class, and when you reached the qualifying, or 11 plus, pupils were split up, and it was the luck of the draw as to your location. Some pupils stayed on at the Ferguson Place School, and others, (including me, unfortunately,) were sent to the Piscy (Episcopalian)) School. This small two storey Victorian building in Manse Lane stood at the top of the long stairs leading from the Music Hall and gas works.

Our classroom was upstairs and had a black stove with a chimney surrounded by a black metal fence in the middle of the room. I can remember nearly fainting after being made to stand by the hot stove for thirty minutes, and getting pushed back roughly to my seat. The heat was unbearable in more ways than one, and the leather belt was used extensively as punishment. All I can say is, the very best part of the experience at the Piscy, was playtime.

Running up the many stairs which lead to Broomhill, was like being on top of the world. We played around the large flagpole till we heard the bell, and were reluctant to enter back into our classroom. Another happy experience at play time was a run down the long stairs, past the gas works and into the heaven which was The Miss Stocks's sweetie shop. Two lovely old dears, one of which was always chewing a sweetie and humming a wee tune.

Sherbet dabs, lucky tatties, (brown flat tatties rolled in cinnamon) , which had wee metal figures inside. My God we could have choked to death! Penny dainties, which you could get in your mouth all at once, milkmaid bars, gobstoppers, butternuts, chewing nuts, and liquorice cartwheels, to name but a few.

God Bless Mrs. Harris, one of our school dinner ladies.

I loved school dinners. Oh boy, they were lovely, except on a Friday when you always got soup and fish. Didn't much care for that! "Where's the pudding?" It was in the days when Catholics didn't eat meat on a Friday, always fish, so the school observed that tradition, as it was a mixed denomination establishment.

What I remember on other days were delicious steak pie, savoury mince, macaroni cheese. Oh, but it was the puddings which I really liked... jam tart and custard, rice and prunes, pink blancmange and the best of all, trifle. I can still visualise it in the metal oblong tray, cut into big squares, with the fluffy cream on top and "hundreds and thousands" decorating the top. Mmmmmmm.

I used to stay behind and help the dinner ladies clear up and made friends with Mrs. Harris, and I got second and sometimes third helpings of the puddings. Yummy. "Oliver Twist, eat yer gruel up, Mrs Harris will give you mair."

Mrs Harris front row left

*The obligatory school photo-Sydney Billy Willie Alec George
Gus David Billy Alec Robin Janice Anita Catherine June
Cecelia Helen Robert Me Margaret Wilma Aileen June Irene
Billy Peter Jack Leslie Drew to name a few.*

Chapter Eleven

The Tattie Howkin'

During the October holidays, the school liaised with the farmers. If you wished, you had the chance to work at the surrounding farms picking potatoes, and getting your very first pay packet.

I wrote a song on the subject which says it all.

Come October Time

By Ray Kelly

Key of D

```
D.                        A.          D
Way back in the 50's, come October time,
G.                        D.              A.
Ye got the chance tae miss the school and make yourselves a
dime
G.                               D
Going tae the tattie howkin' at the farm just up the road,
A.                                       D
```

The tractor picked you up at a spot near your abode.

```
D.                               A.          D
Bumping up the Aberdour Road on a cold and frosty day,
G.              D.          A
Wi' yer bag o' sandwiches, anticipating your pay,
```

G.   D
My pal was a big lad, had twelve pieces under his arm,
A.   D
He had them aw eaten long before we reached the farm.

Chorus
      G.   D.   A.   D
The tattie howkin', the tattie howkin', pickin tatties in the rain,
      G.   D.   A.   D
The tattie howkin', the tattie howkin', never going back again.

        D.   A.   D
The farmer had extra long legs seemed tae reach his oxters
high,
G.   D.   A
As he stepped it oot up the dreels, we aw let oot a sigh,

G.   D
Twigs marked the patch you had tae pick, seemed like half a
mile,
A.   D
But we were young and carefree, ready with our happy smiles.

D.   A.   D
Oh my God, here comes the rain it's mud itsel' and clarty,
G.   D.   A
Canny wait tae dinner time tae have a wee bit party,
G.   D
In the barn sheltering and eating our pieces on jam,
A.   D
Some o' the posher bairns even had some spam!!!

Chorus
      G.   D.   A.   D
The tattie howkin', the tattie howkin' picking' tatties in the rain,
      G.   D.   A.   D
The tattie howkin, the tattie howkin', never going back again.

```
 D                          A.                    D
A Braw pat o' soup, the farmer's wife would sometimes make,
  G          D.                A
The kind that stuck tae yer ribs, 'twas the icing on the cake,
  G                      D
Resting our weary bones on the bales and supping' hot broth,
A.                              D
Half an hour wiz aw we got, it wisnae near enough.
```

```
   D.                              A
There were high jinks between the boys and girls, we new who
        D
fancied who,
G                D        A
Caperin' behind the straw bales, a kiss was shared or two,
G                        D
A stop was soon pit tae that when the farmer shouted "Hey!!!
A.                              D
Get back tae work yea. little buggers, or you'll get no pay".
```

Chorus
```
G                D              A        D
The tattie howkin', the tattie howkin' picking tatties in the rain,
G                D        A        D
The tattie howkin' the tattie howkin', never going back again.
```

```
D                    A        D
The tractor's horn it blew, time tae start again,
G                D          A
Oor backs they were startin' tae hurt, oor legs were racked wi'
pain,
G                D
Roll on four o'clock, when it's lousin' time
A.                              D
 And we'll get a bag o' tatties hame for chips every teatime.
```

D   A.   D
Time passes so slowly, but it's finishing time at last,
G   D   A
Time tae board the trailer, it was hell but it has passed,
G.   D
That is 'till tomorrow, when it aw begins, och aye!
A.   D
Wonder what's for tea the night... hope it's no tattie pie!

Chapter Twelve
Biscuits and God

We roamed around in a gang. Usually a mixed group of boys and girls.

The Salvation Army Hall was at the end of Broomhill Avenue, and we heard through the grapevine that if you went along on a Tuesday night, you got tea and biscuits. "Well, who could resist a biscuit?" Off the gang set in the darkness of evening, along Haugh Road. We always named it The Cowp Road, so called because there was a rubbish tip nearby. There was an enclosure at the bottom of the hill where Mrs. Macadam kept her hens. She would be seen daily, trudging down with a full pail of feeding for them. Also in that area, my uncle Robbie Gilhespie kept his greyhounds. He wasn't my real uncle, but a great family friend. We saved all our tattie peelings for him, which he boiled up for feeding his racing dogs.

The spooky railway tunnel was half way along and there were usually bats flying around the eerie light of the street lamps. The road was prone to flooding at the tunnel and sometimes we crossed the railway to get to school if we were keen to go that particular day, or we used it as an excuse not to go.

The "coo" field was on the right and was where I used to hide when I played truant from school.

Further along was a large grassy area where the Castle Tenants Association would organise gala days for the Castle bairns, with races and prizes. Mr. Hughes would look on from his wee cottage near Ged's Mill. We competed in various races. The three-legged race, wheelbarrow race, egg and spoon race, sack race and many more. We also got a bag of buns. Great fun to be had by all.

Opposite the grassy area was where my future father-in-law kept his hens. We have since learned that some Castle Arabs had stolen some of his hens for their Christmas dinner.

"We know who you are!"

To return to our thought of biscuits, we were full of anticipation for them, but had a wee bit of trepidation too, as we made our way up the half a dozen or so stone steps up to the door of the Salvation Army Hall. "You go in first." "No!" "You go in first."

Eventually this wee group of waifs made their way through the narrow doorway.

There was a lovely smell of fresh polish and rows of benches made with light wood. We were made most welcome and invited to take a seat. There was a Captain, a lady, all dressed in black, apart from a S for Salvation embroidered in red somewhere on her attire, and wearing a beautiful bonnet tied with satin ribbon. We must have become a little rowdy, as we were told to "settle down." A great hush descended, and the Captain made her way onto the raised stage. It began with a prayer, and, as we saw other members of the congregation bowing their heads, we did the same, looking along the line of our pals with our eyes wide open. A lady sat at an organ which was placed at the side. It was quite ornate, with carved features and two rows of black and white keys. There was also a row of knobs, some of which she carefully pulled out in a sort of pattern, and her feet worked what looked like bellows, pushing them up and down. The music began. It was magical. A few lessons of "My cup's full and running over." doing all the actions, soon had us participating with gusto. Tambourines rattled noisily. The song, The Old Rugged Cross was a wee bit too morbid for me. "Oh, how long before we get the biscuits?" We could sense something happening in the kitchen, like water being boiled in an urn for the tea. Then, what we had really come along for... magic... the ladies bringing plates piled high with golden, crispy, fresh biscuits. Rich tea, digestive, ginger snaps, custard creams and a few even with chocolate on. Our eyes were like organ stops! They placed them on a long trestle table covered with white paper. At the other end were the cups and saucers arranged neatly in rows. Oh, they were beautiful. Made of china and oh so posh. We thought our Christmas had arrived. A lady poured out the tea from a large metal teapot, and the party began. The biscuits disappeared like snow off a dyke. The ladies then cleared away the crockery. A few more songs and readings from the Bible, and a last prayer ended the meeting.

We set off into the night feeling a sense of fulfilment. Back along the Cowp Road, into the darkness, to the

Castle area, with the boys jumping out of the indentation at the tunnel trying to scare us. Oh, roll on next Tuesday night. It became our weekly outing. To this day I would never pass a Salvation Army Volunteer standing on a street corner with the collecting can. I'm paying for my biscuits!

Cue for a song…

My Cup's Full and Running Over
By Ray Kelly

D   G   A   D

See the Bonnie ladies, all dressed in black wi' their bonnets tied

        A

with satin ribbon

D   G   A   D   A

Standing in a circle on the beach in the sun, praising the Lord

        D

with song.

        D   G A   D

As the music drifts along, it soon becomes a throng o' bairnies

              A

sitting round the outer edges

D   G   A D

Doing all the actions to the songs with gay abandon and

        A   D

my cup's full and running over

Chorus

G   D

Praise the Lord, I saw the light

D   A

Praise the Salvation Army,

D   G A   D

Good days at the beach, sin was out of reach,

 D   A   D

And my cup's full and running over.

 D   G A   D

The hall was on the corner, and every Tuesday night, us

      A

bairnies made our way,

 D   G A   D

We heard there were free biscuits and a cup o' tea an aw

D   A   D

And my cup's full and running over.

  D   G A D

Noo when we grew up and to the pub did go every Friday night

    A

aboot nine

D   G   A   D

In would come the Sally Army rattlin' their cans and my pint's

A   D

full and running over.

Chorus

G   D

Praise the Lord, I saw the light

D   A

Praise the Salvation Army,

D   G   A   D

'Twas the biscuits that done it, and for that I am so thankit

D   A   D

And my cups full and running over

D   G   A D

Tae tempt us fae sin, noo where tae begin, we were a bunch o'

                A

rascals needing' guidance

    D   G   A   D

Have a read o' the War Cry, it'll help you by and by, and put a

   A

half crown in oor wee tinny.

D   G A D

Noo I'm Auld and grey, I see standing on the corner a Salvation

   A

Army Volunteer

 D   G A D

They'll be glad to hear, I've given up the beer, so I'll put a fiver

A   D

in yer tinny

Chorus

 G   D   A

Praise the Lord, I saw the light, Praise the Salvation Army

 D   G A D

Twas the biscuits that done it, and for that I am so thankit

   D   A   D

And my cups full and running over.

Chapter Thirteen

Keyhole, Liquor and Cigars

We had a particularly lovely friend. We nicknamed him "KEYHOLE", as he only had one eye.

Watery Meg's pub was in The Kirkgate, the road leading up to the historical St Columba's Church. Watery Meg, well the name speaks for itself. Used to water down the drink! Anyhow, there was a wee snug bar, and "Keyhole" although under age, was welcomed in with his pals. You could see green mould in the bottom of the glasses as you drained your pint. Watery Meg would give wee "keyhole" Tom Thumb cigars to smoke to create an ambience in the pub.

There were many drinking establishments in the town, much to the detriment of the wives trying to feed their families. It was a man's world, and women were very rarely seen in the pubs. The Royal Hotel under the railway bridge, would get strippers in on a

Sunday afternoon, fire tartan adorning their legs, Fire tartan was a red pattern you got on your skin, from sitting too close to a hot coal fire. If a man was unlucky enough, his tie would be removed by the stripper, and used as a prop! It would be thrown into the nearby dock afterwards to hide the evidence. An accordionist would be playing until the strippers arrived and a collection would be taken to pay the ladies. One Sunday the collection was taken and the strippers from Edinburgh were not to be seen. The accordionist played faster and faster as the crowd became unruly, demanding their money back. All this was told to me by a third party by the way!

The George Hotel, now the Smugglers in Harbour Place, was next door to my earliest recollection of the place I called home before moving to the Castle. (The fire station occupies the very spot nowadays). We had to enter by a close at the side of the hotel, round the back, then up a wooden stair. The wash house was situated at the rear of the garden, and housed the boiler - a stone built contraption with a cavity at the base where you had to kindle a fire to heat the water. It was shared by four families.

I can remember my father getting into trouble. He

loved to gather the plentiful seafood, parkins and wilks. One day he boiled the wilks in the boiler and the next neighbour to use it got her sheets all covered in wee black bits. I digress… The Pacific Tavern was also in Harbour place. The Green Tree was on the corner, and The Steamboat Tavern faced the dock area where you were free to roam a privilege that is denied to us at the moment One can imagine the scene in the olden days in this dockside area when the sailing ships would arrive, bringing spices and goods from the Orient, which were carted up Spice Row, and the sailors enjoying their refreshments at the numerous watering holes.

The Sailors' home was in Spice Row, a four storey, somewhat foreboding Victorian building, which was a refuge for homeless sailors. There was a tiny shop inside, and it was with fear and dread, when your mother sent you round there for bread or milk. Inside, it was so frugal, like a scene from a Charles Dickens novel. There were large, bare, wooden trestle tables and benches and always a small fire burning in a huge fireplace, with a few of the residents huddled round trying to get some heat into their bodies. You had to press a bell for service at the wee shop, and the glass panel slid along. Once served, you couldn't get out of there quick enough.

The Star Tavern was in close proximity to my birthplace at 18 High Street. The Crown Pub stood on a corner facing the Links. Closing time was 10 p.m. in those days, and you saw many drunk people staggering about the streets, because they had been downing the drink as fast as they could before the bell was rung for closing time. However, around nine o'clock, in would come The Salvation Army. Usually two recruits, selling the War Cry, and rattling their collection tins. To this day, I never pass a Salvation Army person in the street without putting something into their can. I remember "the biscuits."

Des and the Dingoes were our favourite band. They played, among other places, in the Crown and The Orcadia, now The Burntisland Sands Hotel.

The Old Porte Bar stood resplendent at the very end of the High Street overlooking the Links, and there were a further three pubs at the Kirkton. My relation, Trummy Davidson, my gran's nephew, owned the one with the lovely brown varnished tree trunks holding up the entrance porch.

The Greenmount Hotel was another imposing building, and a great favourite. You could get a lovely meal there too. I can remember a fish tank full of lobsters, and you could choose the one you fancied to be cooked to your liking.

The Charene Hotel on the High Street was a great haunt for the teenagers, with discos in the evenings. Special fluorescent lights showed the dandruff on your clothing, and made not so white shirts look dazzling!

Chapter Fourteen

First Dates

The Picture House was an imposing Art Deco building which stood proudly on the High Street, although we didn't really appreciate the architecture at that time. It had a covered canopy where you were protected from the elements and was a great meeting place for first dates. It had enclosed glass sections at either side which showed the pictures of the "forthcoming" and "showing now" pictures. They call them the movies nowadays.

Three sets of swing doors led into the beautiful, mostly cream coloured interior and wide steps led up to the kiosk where you purchased your ticket. On the right was the sweet shop, and then two sets of large brown swing doors. Once inside the usherette checked your ticket by torchlight and ushered you to your seat. You could sit at either side or in the main middle section. The folding seats squeaked as you pulled them down and then made a dull thud, so everyone looked around to see who had just arrived to see the picture.

The picture was projected from the balcony. The balcony was the bees knees. Downstairs were the cheap seats, but the balcony was something else. An impressive staircase on the left led you to a lovely carpeted lounge with low tables and basketwork chairs and beautiful Art Deco stained glass features, before you moved into the darkened balcony. If you got there early, you could marvel at the huge ruched satin curtain which glowed with a golden light.

The Pathe News (News from around the world) preceded the pictures, and began with a cockerel crowing "Cock a Doodle Doo" then sometimes a double feature, two movies with a break in between for ice cream. I was an ice cream lassie for one night. It was too much like hard work totin' that heavy tray though.

It was great fun downstairs. Sweetie papers getting thrown about and our disruptive friend, (we have met him before) shouting "rhubarb" in his loudest voice. I have no idea why he chose that particular word, but it did disrupt the proceedings at the quietest, most crucial part of the picture. He would do this several times, much to the annoyance of Mrs. Cameron, the usherette, who would shine her torch frantically, to determine who the culprit was.

Another meeting place for first dates was in the entrance to the Co-op drapers. It was a shelter against the cold winds which blew across the exposed Links.

The Co-op was a godsend, providing everything from your daily bread, the shoes on your feet, butcher meat, groceries, chemist, and the Store Draper was another gem. It's where the Copper Kettle used to be, now home of the Roasting House Project. It's fun remembering the shops along the High Street in the olden days. In the drapers, the ladies clothes were on the left hanging on racks randomly placed around, and tall glass fronted cabinets with shallow pull out drawers, which were marked with stickers denoting the contents. Nylons, suspender belts, navy blue knickers, brassieres, or BRA's standing for Breast Restraining Apparatus (didn't know that), corsets. liberty bodices, vests. You name it, the store had everything you could ever wish for. The gents department was on the right. I won't say anything about the men's clothes – too boring.

A staircase led upstairs to the hardware department, and halfway up the stairs on a landing, a cardboard cutout of a teddy bear greeted you, advertising bear brand nylon stockings.

You could get anything from the Co-op without paying there and then. Your mother joined the Mutuality Club and paid in so much every week. Most families couldn't afford to purchase goods outright, so it was a good way to get custom and benefited everyone.

It was called "ON TICK!"

The freezing shelters on the Links provided a place for the young couples to meet and have a wee snog to keep warm, and probably have the first taste of the demon drink as they slugged out of a wine or sherry bottle.

The Swimming Club premises provided a great rendezvous for us youngsters. They were situated at the top of the Kirkgate near the Parish Church of St Columba. It was underground and you entered down a flight of steps. There was a jukebox playing all the latest 1950s songs. Bill Halley and the Comets released a song in 1954, which was the first rock and roll music to be heard. Rock around the Clock was a favourite. The Palace Picture House in Burntisland wouldn't screen the movie, but the Kinghorn picture house did and there was a riot with chairs being ripped off the floor as the kids went wild. The swimming club was where the first taste of a Woodbine cigarette was sampled, with lots of coughing ensuing. The best chat line ever was when my future husband came over and said, "how about teaching me to jive?" There was a church meeting place down in the basement too, and I remember what used to be an old picture house upstairs, which was then used as a gym. This is where we used to swing on the parallel bars.

Just around the corner in East Leven Street was the SWRI (Scottish Women's Rural Institute) hall. A damp wee hall, but there was always a roaring fire lit to welcome the members. We had many happy meetings there, practising for concerts and being entertained by visiting Rurals, and best of all, the delicious home baking provided by the talented members. "Big Bill" kept his pigeons below the hall.

S.W.R.I. That's entertainment, with Isa Duncanson

The church, which was opposite, was a central meeting place in the town with Sunday School, and many events taking place in the large adjacent halls.

The church itself had an escape staircase at the rear, so that the sailors could exit quietly, and quickly make their way back to their ships docked in the harbour. A lane ran between the Church and the halls, and led to a quiet area overlooking the harbour. This was a favourite haunt of young lovers and was aptly named "Lovers Lane."

The Palais de Dance in Manse Lane was our local dance hall. It was pretty busy in those days, with many famous bands appearing. It had great big comfy couches and lights sunk into the floor. Many first dates began in good old Burntisland Palais.

Coming along Manse Lane after a party at Burntisland Palais

Quite a few of the Castle bairns attended Alice Robson's dancing, and concerts by her pupils were sometimes performed in the Palais. My friend Kathleen and I, both aged 9, and resplendent in our wee kilts, made by our mothers, were performing the sword dance. We were very nervous as there was a large audience. First, one of my swords went swirling across the floor, followed swiftly by the other. I was devastated!

The Spinster
By Ray Kelly

```
E                                    E7
```
I met wi' a wee laudie, he asked me for a date,
```
   A                           E
```
I telt him I was winchin', had to hurry or I'd be late
```
      B7                              A
```
He kept phoning, I was groaning, but the phone it wouldn't stop,
```
   E                            B7              E
```
I consented, he was contented, seven o'clock at the Co-op shop.

```
      E.                                      E7
```
I was looking' kind o' fancy, my beehive hair was lookin great,
```
      A                          E
```
I was running in my high heels, can't be late for my first date

```
      B7                          A
```
Then I saw him roond the corner, all dressed up in teddy boy gear,
```
   E                              B7
```
Winklepickers, drainpipe troosers, and clutching a bottle of
```
E
```
beer.

```
      E
```
He was smoking', I'm no joking, drawin' woodbine in his

E7
mooth,

     A   E
I couldn't see him for the fag reek, this teddy boy was so
uncouth
  B7.   A
I remember some advice that my mother gave to me,
         E.   B7   E
"Ma wee lass, mind and keep your hand, on yer halfpenny."

       E   E7
 I didnae like him, I didnae like him, so I turned and I did run,
     A   E
I wiz goin' back to safety, tae ma hoose and tae ma mum
    B7   A
So the moral of this story, be a good girl and stay away,
         E   B7   E
From the prancers and the chancers, who happen by your way.
     E
Just ignore them, leave them hingin', plenty more fish in the
  E7
sea,

     A   E
Canny whack it, just stay crabbit', and be a spinster just like me
     B7.   A
Just ignore them, leave them hingin', plenty more fish in the sea
38   E.   B7.   E
Canny whack it, just stay crabbit, and be a spinster just like me

Chapter Fifteen

Jobs for All

There was plenty of work for our mothers, mainly in Kirkcaldy, at either the linen factory or the factory which made delicious white chocolate drops. I have a vision of the white linen dish towels with the coloured stripe running across them!

The Factory Girls
By Ray Kelly

G.   Em.   Am. D.   G.   Em.   Am.   D
Time to rise, get out of bed, the house is cold, stay cosy instead
G.   Em.   Am.   D.   G.   Em.   Am.   D
Icy cold water to wake me up, a cup of tea to quickly sup
G. Em. Am. D.   G. Em. Am. D
Hair in rollers, headscarves on, the daily ritual has begun,
G.   Em.   Am.   D. G.   Em. Am.   D
Off to the factory to make their pay, factory girls grafting all day.

Chorus
     C.   C7
The girls, the girls, the factory girls,
G.   G7
The girls, the girls, the factory girls,
C
Working their fingers to the bone,
D   A   D
Just can't wait 'till they get home

G.   Em.   Am. D.   G. Em.   Am.   D
Through the black iron gates, got to run, or they'll be late
G.   Em.   Am.   D.   G.   Em. Am. D
Clocking in and clocking out, is this what life is all about?

G.   Em.   Am. D.   G.   Em. Am.   G
The boss is watching all the time, to see if we are talking in line
G.   Em.   Am. D.   G.   Em.   Am.
Five minute break is all we get, that boss is such an awful
G
threat.

Chorus
    C.   C7
The girls, the girls, the factory girls,
G.   G7
The girls, the girls, the factory girls,
C
Working their fingers to the bone,
D.   A.   D
Just can't wait 'till they get home

G.   Em. Am.   D. G.   Em.   Am.   D
Ten hour shift has been done, now Is the time to have some fun
G.   Em.   Am.   D.   G.   Em.
Tired and weary, girls go home, the day has just been
Am.   D
monochrome
G.   Em. Am.   D.   G.   Em. Am.   D
The evening out, to the dance, perhaps it will bring romance
G.   Em. Am.   D.   G.   Em.   Am.
Curlers out, looking good, homemade dress don't look like it
  D
should

G.   Em.   Am. D.   G.   Em.   Am.
Lipstick on for the dance tonight, factory girls are a charming
 D
sight,
G.   Em.   Am.   D. G.   Em.   Am. D
To the village hall they go, Time to forget their life of woe
G.   Em. Am. D. G.   Em.
The band strikes up to a jazzy beat, makes them want to
 Am   D
tap their feet
G.   Em.   Am.   D.   G.   Em.   .
Boys on one side, girls on the other, romance waiting
   Am.   D
to be discovered.

Chorus
     C.   C7
The girls, the girls, the factory girls,
G.   G7
The girls, the girls, the factory girls,
C
Working their fingers to the bone,
D.   A.   D
Just can't wait 'till they get home

.

The teenagers left school at 15 and stepped right into
a job. The schools liaised with different companies
and arranged interviews with the pupils.

Things were so very different in those days and I feel so lucky to have been born at the right time. The good old days indeed. It's such a shame to see young folk struggling to get a decent job nowadays, even if they have excellent qualifications.

In the last few weeks of the course, the interviews for various office jobs were taking place and I was sent to Nairns the linoleum people in Kirkcaldy, for an interview for an office job. You got a test, and one of the questions was on spelling... Oh well, I made a mess of that one! Needless to say, I didn't get the job.

I've loved every job I've had, firstly in various offices, then, after having our family, reverting to floristry and being self-employed. I prepared flowers for weddings and other occasions. It was hard work too, often travelling to Glasgow flower market at 5 a.m.

My very first permanent job was in the offices of Burntisland Shipbuilding Company Limited, then I moved on to Carnegie and Grant, grain merchants, then finally settled in the Burgh Chamberlain's Office for many years. Duties there involved collecting rents and rates, typing the Births, Deaths and Marriages

Certificates, and bookkeeping. "The Lavvy Man" used to arrive early on a Monday morning with the takings from the toilets at the Porte! It was a penny a pee!

The Lavvy Man
By Ray Kelly

```
        G.                          C     G
When I worked in the cooncil offices, a long time ago
        C.        G.              D.              D7
On a Monday morn at ten o'clock the lavvy man would show
        G                        C.
Was his job tae clean the ladies lavvies, it cost a penny you
  G
know
    C              G.                      D.
It went in the slot of a polished brass box, and the pee, well it
        G
would flow
C.                      G
On the seat, doon the pan, running under the door
      D.                              G
Running aff the toilet paper, making puddles on the floor
C.                      G
Running doon their stockings, creating quite a stink
      D.                              G
Then tryin' tae wash it aff in the white cracked Shanks's sink
```

Chorus

```
        C.                      G
The lavvy man, the lavvy man, the man who cleans the lavvies
        D.
A champion in that underground sewer, he was downright
```

D
savvy

    C.   G

He works doon there from nine 'till five, scrubbing' aw the pee

    D.   G

Someone's got tae dae it, just glad it wiznae me

G.   C.   G

The toilets they were underground, red tiles everywhere,

    C.   G.   D.   D7

The seats a sturdy oval for the fat bums to rest there

    G   C

The paper came oot sheet by sheet, from a slot in a box on the

 G

wall

    C.   G.   D.   G

The shiny stuff called Izal, which wiznae absorbent at all

    C.   G   .

Tae flush it, there hung a chain wi' a ceramic bit on the end

      D.   G

It was awfy posh, in blue and white tae send yer jobbies round

the bend

    C.   G

The cistern high took ages tae fill, one drop at a time

        D.

 If the toilet was blocked and wouldn't flush, that man to the

        G

rescue came.

Chorus

   C.   G

The lavvy man, the lavvy man, the man who cleans the lavvies

   D.

A champion in that underground sewer, he was downright

   D

savvy

   C.   G

He works doon there from nine 'till five, scrubbing' aw the pee

   D.   G

Someone's got tae dae it, just glad it wiznae me

      C.   G

The lavvy man spent aw weekend counting the piles o' pennies

D   D7

Rolling them in the Sunday Post and the pennies they were

 G

many

    C.   G

They smelled o' disinfectant t'was a wonder I wiznae ill

    D.   G.

'Twas me who had tae count them and put them in the till.

    C.   G.

A penny a pee, a penny a pee, the lavvy man and me

D.   G

Well documented for posterity.

After having our family, I reverted to floristry and was self-employed, creating flowers for weddings and other occasions. Sitting various tests to become an Area Demonstrator was fun, and you didn't always pass the first time. It was a case of try, try, try again. My persistence paid off eventually, as I qualified as a N.A.F.A.S. (National Association of Flower Arrangement Societies) National Demonstrator. There were only five of us in the whole of Scotland.

This meant a lot of travelling, from Orkney to Cornwall, and all places in between, sometimes on a tour which took you each day to a different flower club. Many miles were covered. It was lovely meeting all the members.

Careful planning was imperative. Four days' worth of flowers, foliage, accessories, and containers were all loaded into the car and off you went to entertain the ladies and a few gents. There could be 20 or 200 in the audience. The roads were a lot quieter back in the 1960s and 1970s, and three times round the roundabout wasn't unusual, deciding what turn off to take to get to the destination - no sat navs in those days.

I did a lot of work for the rural SWRI (Scottish Women's Rural Institute) back then, judging their floral art competitions and teaching their members, as well as teaching flower arranging in night school.

I had a lovely invitation to go to Orkney to give a demonstration and classes to the rural members over 4 days. "You'll be flying from Edinburgh and staying with Phoebe at her farmhouse." This all sounded wonderful.

Everything packed in boxes, my husband accompanied me to the airport. From the viewing platform I could see a big plane sitting on the tarmac. Ah, but it was not to be. I was told, "this is your plane." … a wee 12 seater, hidden round the corner. It was prop driven, wires showing inside – a shoogly wee bone shaker. Oh dear, it was so scary. However, I landed in one piece for the work ahead. It was hard work, but most enjoyable, and the Orcadians are such lovely people.

It was after classes morning and afternoon, then a demonstration at night, that I arrived back at Phoebe's farmhouse, pretty exhausted, but happy. Oh, a relaxing bath was on the cards. Turn on the taps, in goes the bubble bath. I needed this. Immersed and relaxed after a busy day, I noticed a couple of buttons on the side of the bath, so being inquisitive, I pressed one, and lo and behold, the water began to bubble. "Oh my God, we didn't have anything so posh up the Castle." "This is wonderful." Ah, but the foam began to bubble too. The bubbles continued to rise until they were a foot above the rim of the bath. Have you ever tried to get rid of soapy suds? So much for a relaxing time.

What an adventure for the wee lassie who spent her childhood years up the Castle.

I was remembering too, with fear and trepidation that I still had to make the flight back to Edinburgh. As there was time to spare, the young lady pilot said, "I'll take you on a flight around Ronaldsay." "Oh dear, I just wanted to go home." All the bairns from Rossend Terrace have done well for themselves, because of the wonderful childhood we had, gaining the experience needed to survive in life. Thanks also to our parents, who worked hard to make ends meet.

My lovely mother Meg, who worked tirelessly to give us a childhood worth remembering…

My Mum Meg
A poem by Ray Kelly

My mum she was loving and kind,
With tending us kids on her mind,
She would make do and mend, stipple walls, make
good friends,
And I cherish her memory so well.

In the kitchen a whizz, making soup for us kids,
Then away helping others to cope,
Whilst we kids were a playing along the Monks' Walk
And slidin' down the slippy slope.

With the money she made being a home help,
She would take us to Butlin's and Blackpool,
And often as not on a Sunday so super,
On a mystery tour tae Bonny Cupar.

A talented mum knitting cardigans fine,
Making dresses wi polka dots on them,
Playing the squeeze box, and always upbeat,
In my heart for ever and ever.

My mum Meg

Chapter Sixteen

Reminiscence

My grandparents lived above Knox's paper shop and MacRae Forbes the Jeweller. I was a bit scared of my grandfather, and always on my best behaviour when I visited. He worked as an engine driver on the railway, shunting engines across the Forth Railway Bridge. He gets a mention in the Roll of Honour, Book of Heroes, which is housed in the Andrew Carnegie Birthplace in Dunfermline. There are three leather bound volumes, beautifully illuminated and hand inscribed. Once, he bravely rescued someone from the railway line just moments before the train approached.

I can remember, it was an annual occurrence, on New Year's Day, and a jolly day to remember, when all the Thomson relations gathered together to celebrate the New Year.. My dad Jock, Uncle Charlie, wee Charlie and Dorothea, Auntie Christie, Auntie Jeannie, my twin sisters Sandra and Sheila and myself were all there.

All of the meat was bought from the Co-op butcher, always salt beef, brisket, a ham and an ox tongue, which was placed in a bowl after cooking, with a plate and heavy weight on top.

The big table would be set in the front room. It was a lovely big room, with a piano on the wall between the two windows and a welcoming fire burning in the Robert Adam fireplace.

The meal was to be at two o'clock. The tattles were ready, the steak pie and everything else, but no sign of the men who were celebrating the New Year in The Star Tavern. We were starving, and still no sign, as we hung out the windows, watching intently for our dad and uncle to come staggering up the High Street. Eventually they arrived, in high "spirits" indeed, and entertained us with laughter and fun, as we sat at the table awaiting our meal. Afterwards, Auntie Jeannie would play the piano. "Oh my was she good, just like Winifred Atwell" as she tinkled the ivories. What fabulous New Year's Days we had at my grandparents.

My grandparents' house was situated in a grand location on the High Street. The perfect viewing platform to witness the marvellous spectacle of Parade Day in Burntisland. We sat at the open windows, our legs resting on the wooden box type affairs which housed the sun canopies for MacRae Forbes the Jeweller and Knox's paper shop. The parade gathered in front of the half-moon by the shipyard. The judging took place here, and almost all the different organisations in the town would hire lorries and transform them according to the theme which was chosen each year. Individuals took part also. I participated, and one year, won first prize. My mum dressed me up as "Annie Get Your Gun!"

Go get 'em Annie!

Once the judging was completed, the parade set off under the railway bridge and up the High Street, with the Burntisland Pipe Band leading the procession. I still get goosebumps when I hear the pipes and drums. The day was full of vibrancy and fun, with individuals rattling cans and buckets and shaking large brown blankets for donations for the various committees.

The twins on parade day

Money would be thrown from the windows and by the crowds lining the pavements, hoping their aim would be successful. The parade continued up Cromwell Road, along Kirkton Road and back along Broomhill Avenue, culminating at the Links.

Our flat in Harbour Place, above the Globe Tavern, (it's where the Fire Station is now), looked out onto the fantastic railway bridge, where we would watch the steam trains passing, emitting thick black smoke into the atmosphere. Occasionally we had a trip in the train, the carriages being all individual. As you opened the door, you saw the carriage had two long upholstered seats which could hold six passengers. Above was the luggage rack, made from a thick string like material. No health and safety back then as we hung out of the carriage window, getting our faces covered in soot from the engine. A thick leather strap was used to open the window and was secured by placing a hole in the strap onto a metal pin.

The bottom of the High Street was the turning point for Alexander's Bluebird buses, and the starting point for any journeys. The toilets were situated under the bridge. If you walked under the bridge, this led along by the shipyard. My grandparents, before moving to that lovely house on the High Street, stayed in the wee cottage at the bottom of the half moon, with Rossend Castle towering high above.

My Grandfather had an allotment there. "Digging for Victory" was a Second World War slogan, encouraging folks to grow their own fruit and vegetables, but people kept allotments after the war as well and I remember allotments were everywhere. My grandfather's allotment had a high stone wall backing it with a raised planting area in front, and I loved when he took me along to help. You had to walk up some wooden steps to reach the garden. I imagine this used to be the kitchen garden for Rossend Castle, ideally facing south, with the stone wall behind which would retain the heat. It was amazing to see the wonderfully rich black soil, with the vegetables growing in perfect rows. Beetroot, carrots, onions and potatoes. There was a plant, I call it apple ringy, with a soft feathery grey foliage, which, when rubbed between your fingers, had a lovely distinct smell. I have it in my garden, and it reminds me of the happy sunny days spent at my grandfather's allotment. I can still smell the invasive mint too. There were stone steps leading up to a locked gate and beyond the castle grounds.

On the subject of toilets… if you were having a happy day at the beach, it was best to choose your spot, near to the Beach Tea Rooms as this was where the toilets were. This area of the beach was also where the Salvation Army gathered in a circle to sing their songs. Mr. and Mrs. Souter owned the Tea Rooms, and there were also baths beside the toilets, which were busy in those days, as not many people even had a bath at home. The Tea Room was where you went for your sweets and ice cream, if you had any pocket money, but we didn't get inside. Instead, a window was opened, and you had to queue outside to be served.

At one point, there were eleven sets of twins in Rossend Terrace. I always had to look after my younger twin sisters, when my parents were working. It was a pain – every photograph of us together, my face was tripping me! I usually took them to the bathing pool or the beach, in a twin pram covered in blue rexine. One fine day at the beach could have ended in disaster!

The twins were happily playing on the beach, and I

began to lose interest in the job I was supposed to be doing – looking after them. Next thing I noticed, they had crawled across the sand, down to the shoreline, and were up to their waists in the tide, as they held onto Shanks, the boatman's wooden gangway! I was relieved that I had noticed in time.

There was always a queue to board the boats and have a leisure cruise around the bay. Perhaps the twins had fancied a wee sail.

A group of childhood friends meet up once a year to take a nostalgic walk and retrace our steps from Rossend Castle, along the Monks walk to Rossend Point and the Breakwater, reminiscing about the happy days of our youth. We were oh so fortunate to have enjoyed our many adventures and lived to tell the tale.

I am finishing this story about childhood and youth, by giving you a song which says it all…

Childhood pals and happy memories

Top: Setting off on one of our nostalgic walks
Bottom: granddaughters Maisie, and Fern

In the red phone box

Starleyburn picnic
Don't forget the vinegar!

The twins on the Links
Anyone for cricket?

The Good Old Days
By Ray Kelly

G.   C.   G.
Clothes on our backs, sand shoes on our feet, bread in oor
D
bellies
G.   C.   D.   G
we were so poor in the good old days, didn't even have a telly
G.   C.   G.   D
Out all day from the crack of dawn, slipping' and a slidin'
G.   C.   D.
Running wild wi' the wind in oor hair, oor class we weren't
 G
hidin'

Chorus
  C.   G.   D.   G
The good old days, the good old days, everything to live for
  C.   G.   D.
Nae seat in oor breeks claes we wore for weeks and nae herm
   G
did it dae us

G.   C. G.   D
Rag man comin' roond the hooses wi his horse and cart
G.   C.   D.   G
Balloons galore from the rag man and a carrot for his nag

G.   C.   G   D
Goin' crabbin' wi' ma faither, turning' ower the rocks wi' a cleek

G.   C.   D.   G
Bilin' up the parkins and howkin' oot the meat

Chorus
    C.   G.   D.   G
The good old days, the good old days, everything to live for
    C.   G.   D.
Nae seat in oor breeks claes we wore for weeks and nae herm
    G
did it dae us

    G.   C.   G.   D
Store baker comin' roond too, fag hingin' oot his mooth
G.   C.   D.   G
It was a race by all the residents when his horse it had a poo
    G.   C.   G.   D
It was so good for the garden, that manure so steamy and hot
    G.   C.   D.   G
Mrs.Gow had the biggest totties, wi' her shovel she got the lot

G.   C.   G.
Going up the brae empty handed, tae ma hoose and tae ma
D
mum
G.   C.   D.   G
Because the shovel was empty, got a good crack on the bum
    G.   C.   G.   D
I hadn't run hard enough and that woman she beat me
    G.   C.   D.   G
She'll no' beat me tomorrow, I'll win just wait and see
    G.   C.   G.   D
To reminisce on your childhood Is soothing to the soul

```
   G.                      C.     D.                G
Poor as church mice but so happy I cherish these years so
   G.               C.            G.          D
To reminisce on your childhood is soothing to the soul
 G.                            C.     D.                G
Poor as church mice but so happy, I cherish these years so.
```

Remembering our adventures and the friendships that were made

UP THE CASTLE AND BEYOND